YOUR KNOWLEDGE HAS VALUE

AF136900

- We will publish your bachelor's and
  master's thesis, essays and papers

- Your own eBook and book -
  sold worldwide in all relevant shops

- Earn money with each sale

Upload your text at www.GRIN.com
and publish for free

Bibliographic information published by the German National Library:

The German National Library lists this publication in the National Bibliography; detailed bibliographic data are available on the Internet at http://dnb.dnb.de .

Imprint:

Copyright © 2018 GRIN Verlag
Print and binding: Books on Demand GmbH, Norderstedt Germany
ISBN: 9783346053374

This book at GRIN:

https://www.grin.com/document/505644

Melih Aracli

Green Business Process Management. Usage of Existing and New Tools for Achieving the Ecological Goals

GRIN Verlag

GRIN - Your knowledge has value

Since its foundation in 1998, GRIN has specialized in publishing academic texts by students, college teachers and other academics as e-book and printed book. The website www.grin.com is an ideal platform for presenting term papers, final papers, scientific essays, dissertations and specialist books.

Visit us on the internet:

http://www.grin.com/

http://www.facebook.com/grincom

http://www.twitter.com/grin_com

Melih Aracli

Green Business Process Management

Seminar Thesis
in the context of the seminar "Green IS Research"

at the Chair for Information Systems and Information Management
(Westfälische Wilhelms-Universität, Münster)

Date of Submission: 2018-08-10

Content

Figures

Tables

Abbreviations

ABC	Activity Based Costing
BPM	Business Process Management
BPS	Business Process Simulation
CMM	Capability Maturity Model
C02	Carbon dioxide
CPM	Critical Path Method
E-BP	Energy-Aware Business Process
EWP	Ecological Workflow Pattern
GBPM	Green Business Process Management
GHG	Greenhouse Gas
GIS	Geographic Information Systems
GPI	Green Performance Indicator
ICT	Information and Communcation Technology
IS	Information Systems
QoS	Quality of Service

1   Business Process Management in the Green IS Domain

Companies have been looking at sustainability for several decades, recognizing that by reducing pollution they can also maximize their profits. Thus, sustainability in the field of Information Systems (IS) is becoming increasingly important as topics like Green IS and IT are addressed. These deal with the reduction of IT consumption and emissions because of the implementation of more sustainable business activities (Watson et al. 2010). However, this raises the requirement for approaches in the field of Business Process Management. Research and practice lacked an appropriate approach to connect these two areas of Green IS and BPM, which is why the notion of Green Business Process Management was introduced. Experts are developing instruments and techniques whose primary objective is to integrate sustainability into the different phases of the business process Lifecycle so that more ecological processes can be realized. Such approaches help organizations in defining their optimal business strategies regarding the four dimensions of time, quality, flexibility, cost and now adding the aspect of environment (Opitz et al. 2014, p. 3808).

However, according to HOUY ET AL. (2010, p. 509), the research field of Green BPM "has to examine whether existing tools can be adapted or new ones have to be developed". The objective of this seminar thesis is to find an answer towards this problem. For this reason, the research question "Do Green BPM approaches involve the adaptation of existing tools and techniques or the introduction of new ones in order to achieve their ecological goals?" is going to be examined during the different stages of this thesis.

In order to do so, the thesis is structured as follows. First, the current state of research regarding more sustainable business processes, approaches in the domain of Business Process Management and a framework for integrating the approaches are reviewed, which motivate the specific research question (Section 2). To answer this question, the methodology of this work is introduced in the following (Section 3). Thereafter, an analysis of current Green BPM tools and techniques and how they fit into an adapted (Green) BPM Lifecycle are presented, followed by a brief classification of the approaches in relation to their primary objectives (Section 4). Moreover, a discussion of these results (Section 5) precedes the final conclusion (Section 6).

2 From BPM to Sustainability

In the following subsection a theoretical background on the concepts of BPM, Green IS and also the rise of Green BPM is provided. Thereafter, approaches of the traditional BPM field are shown which derives the importance for a BPM Lifecycle as a framework considering the allocation of different BPM tools and techniques.

2.1 Business Process Management and Green IS

Due to the ever increasing globalization and the associated competition, companies had to adjust to the ever changing needs of customers. These continuous adjustments eventually led to the introduction of a management approach that supported organizational processes in companies called Business Process Management (BPM) (Scheer and Hoffmann 2015, pp. 351). This process-oriented practice contains a whole range of different definitions in literature. Therefore, KARAGIANNIS (2013, p. 1) describes BPM as "a set of structured methods and technologies for managing and transforming organizational operations". ROHLOFF (2011, p. 383) clarifies "a management practice which encompasses all activities of identification, definition, analysis, design, execution, monitoring & measurement, and continuous improvement of business processes." In general, BPM is seen as the discipline that applies different approaches to the organizations processes in order to improve their business activities by increasing flexibility, reducing costs, saving time and improving quality (Hammer and Champy 1993). However, the further adjustments in the market show that these four dimensions are no longer sufficient to stand up against the competition. Raw materials are becoming increasingly scarce, people's living standards are changing and also the requirements of customers. Consequently, the management of a company must adapt its business processes to meet the rising importance of sustainability in organizational context (Seidel et al. 2012, p. 4). For this reason, the research area of BPM has to adapt its techniques and tools to dedicated requirements. Due to strong interdependence between environmental impact and resource usage, IS and the IT infrastructure have also to be taken into account, defined under the term of Green IS which refers to "an integrated and cooperating set of people, processes, software, and information technologies to support individual, organizational, or societal goals" (Watson et al. 2010, p. 24). As an intersection of the conventional BPM and Green IS, the new field of Green Business Process Management or simply Green BPM has raised (Opitz et al. 2014). It is seen as "the sum of all IS-supported management activities that help to monitor and reduce the environmental impact of business processes in their design, improvement, implementation or operation stages, as well as lead to cultural change within the process Lifecycle" (Opitz et al. 2012, p. 3812). When improving process activities, Green BPM does not only consider the optimization of existing processes, but also the negative environmental impact of these business processes. The environmental objectives may be the reduction of energy and material flows as well as the reduction of emissions and waste (Seidel et al. 2012). By adding the aspect of sustainability into the Devil's Quadrangle introduced by MANSAR AND REIJERS (2005), which declines the four dimensions of successful Business Process Management, it is transformed into a Devil's Pentagon (Fig. 1):

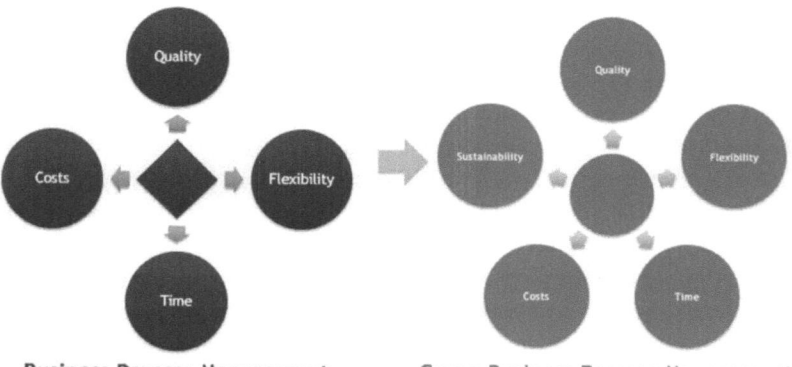

Business Process Management   Green Business Process Management

Seidel et al. (2012), p. 4

Fig. 1   Transformation from Devil's Quadrangle to Pentagon

It is particularly clear that the enlargement to an ecological dimension can also cause conflicts between the different dimensions. For instance, the use of environmentally sustainable products can lead to better quality but with higher costs. In other cases, business processes have to be executed within a certain period of time, which can also result in higher costs. This is precisely why Green BPM approaches must demonstrate flexibility and adaptability in order to realize agile process activities. Under certain circumstances, improving time efficiency is more important for achieving the objective than natural resource efficiency. Taking into account the extended dimension of optimization, the transformation of traditional BPM towards Green BPM needs to be considered at different levels (Ghose et al. 2010).

2.2   Approaches in the field of BPM

In the BPM perspective, an approach refers to a wide range of sub-concepts related to a strategic understanding of the major subject Business Process Management. In addition, the term "approach" is used in the context of a broad definition of BPM (Møller et al. 2008). The usage and definition of BPM in literature is often difficult to turn it into something which is easy in implementation. Due to the difficulties of generalization, a more holistic approach is pursued (Pritchard and Armistead 1999). On the other hand, it is expected that a holistic BPM approach is needed to capture all the relevant parties, not just solving the enterprise vulnerability or using it for the IT department itself (Redshaw 2005, p. 15). Of course, this difference in approach gives different perceptions and views of BPM. Although the BPM literature is not exhaustive, it describes the scope and definition that should be collected (Lee and Dale 1998). Because of the different perceptions of BPM and the conflicts that arise, understanding BPM might refer to the use of BPM instead of understanding the potential and needs for process thinking. This lack of process competencies in the workforce leads to different process management approaches across the organization and is therefore crucial in eliminating the added value of the company's BPM thinking (Melenovsky 2006, p. 6).

Over the last years, a large number of approaches have been proposed to support BPM or certain phases of it. Popular examples are in the area of Business Process Modelling and methods for reengineering the business processes (Bucher et al. 2015, p. 204). But there are also approaches which apply Activity Based Costing based on STAUBUS (1971) to BPM, where the focus lies on the definition of actual costs as the starting point for the internal cost allocation and the external cost calculation by defining a transparent activity based costing (Karagiannis 2013, p. 9).

VOM BROCKE AND MENDLING (2018) proposed a set of 31 cases which relate to different phases of the BPM Lifecycle (see Section 2.3). Five of these cases deal with process identification, seven relate to process discovery, two report process analysis, eight focus on process redesign, six involve process implementation and three deal with process monitoring and controlling (Fig. 3).

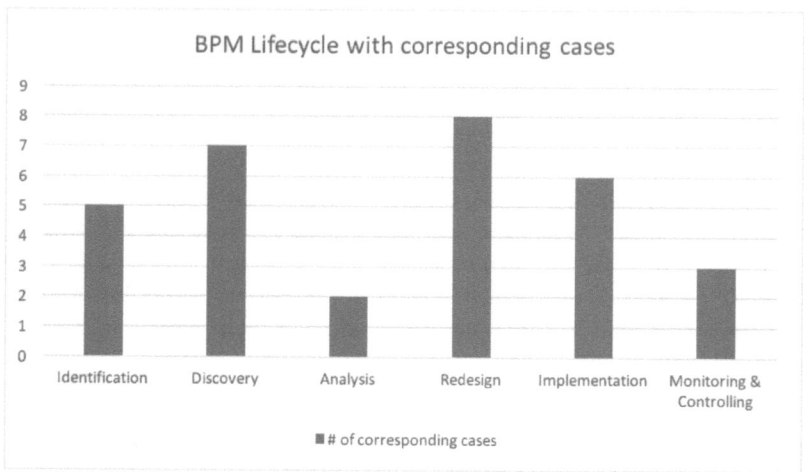

vom Brocke and Mendling (2018), p. 10

Fig. 2   BPM Lifecycle with corresponding cases

Although only two cases mainly contribute to process analysis, most cases involve process analysis by discussing process redesign. This interaction of the two phases demonstrates that the cases went beyond process analysis and saw analysis as a means of iterative process improvement. These cases then help to surpass the knowledge that previous BPM research has reported on organizations whose BPM initiatives have failed because they focused too much on process analysis and did not deliver business value through actual process improvement (vom Brocke et al. 2014).

2.3   BPM Lifecycle

In order to be able to use BPM in a targeted manner, it is necessary to identify processes that are relevant to the actual problem statement, evaluate the scope of these processes, and establish relationships between these processes. In the literature, this initial phase is often referred as *process identification*. This phase results in a process architecture that represents the different relationships between various processes. Once the processes are identified, the next phase deals with the detailed understanding of the business process, which is called *process discovery*. From this, one or more as-is process models are derived, which should reflect the understanding of the employees in the company regarding the executable work. The primary goal of these process models are to facilitate communication between the involved stakeholders. However, problems may occur because of miscommunication, technical errors or lack of information. Only if the root causes of such inconsistencies are identified, classified and understood, the main problems may be resolved. The identification and evaluation of possible challenges and problem areas for process improvement culminate in the *analysis phase*. Once the problem areas are identified through potential remedial action, the processes can be *redesigned*. Such a revised version supports a to-be process that addresses the problems of the as-is process. This creates a connecting factor to the analysis phase since there are several redesign options that can be analysed, so that the best option can be chosen at the end. Thereafter, the implementation phase follows by implementing the necessary information systems in order to capture and track activities so that the to-be process can ultimately be executed. As the implemented business process does not immediately meet the expectations, some adjustments are expected. For this reason, processes have to be monitored and the collected data reviewed in order to make adjustments as well as better control of the process execution. This happens in the *process monitoring and controlling phase*, which is of particular value since solving the problem is not enough to implement successful processes. The activities have to be continuously monitored and improved so that degradation can be avoided. All of these phases are part of the BPM Lifecycle which helps to clarify the immense importance of technology in BPM. In this occasion, technology is considered as a key component to improve business processes (Dumas et al. 2013).

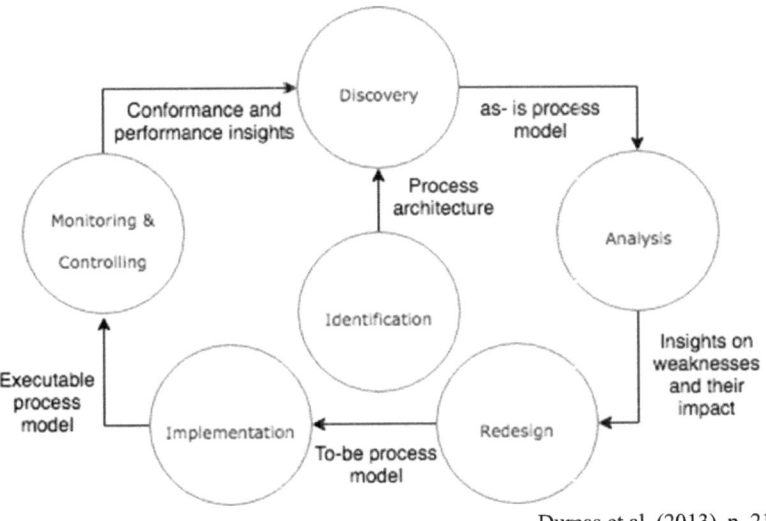

Dumas et al. (2013), p. 21

Fig. 3   BPM Lifecycle

3   Methodology

To accomplish the research objective, a structured literature review following the principles of WEBSTER AND WATSON (2002) have been conducted and applied according the methods of LEVY AND J. ELLIS (2006) in the first step since they take the essential characteristics of reproducibility, systematics and explicitness of a literature search into account and include a framework for a systematic approach to work. The research subject can be attributed to three different literature domains: Green BPM as the primary subject and its intersections of Green IS and BPM. To identify search terms relevant for the study, keywords, variations and word-stems in relation to the three areas were searched in a set of publications in well known IS journals and high quality conferences, since most IS and BPM publications are published in these channels, including the Association for Information Systems (AIS), the Business Process Management Journal (BPMJ) as well as top BPM and IS community conferences such as ECIS, ICIS, ACIS, PACIS, AMCIS and BPM. Not all papers do directly mention the term of Green BPM approaches, but are still focusing on approaches in the field of BPM and sustainability (e.g. such as energy, emission, ecological, carbon-footprint). By broadening the search terms and combining them with Boolean operators, additional papers used by IS and BPM researchers could be identified for the further analysis. Therefore, these terms were also included in the search process using different databases such as Google Scholar, IEEE Xplore, ACM Digital Library, Springer Link and EBSCOhost. In order to achieve a higher relevance of the respective articles, the search in all databases was reduced to contributions published after 2009 thus Green BPM played a significant role from that point on (Ghose et al. 2010). Furthermore, the papers were chosen according to their title and abstract. Through the identification process of the most regular used Green BPM terms in IS and BPM publications, a list of relevant keywords and their potential combinations is derived (see Appendix). Afterwards, iterative forward and backward searches were performed in order to explore bibliographic references and authors in other publications.

In the further step, a relevant framework needed to be found in order to put the different approaches regarding Green BPM in a structured manner and analysing their purpose. Performing a second literature review, the BPM Lifecycle seemed to be the most appropriate one. Therefore, the founded results from the first stage were mapped into the Lifecycle so that implications for the research objective could be derived. The particular allocation is made in accordance with the used tools and techniques and their matching accuracy with respect to the different phases of the BPM Lifecycle.

4   Analysis of Green BPM tools and techniques

This chapter constitutes the main part of this thesis. First, the main findings with regard to the Green Business Process Management approaches are presented in order to investigate the current stage-of-the-art. Based on these findings, the named approaches are put into the Business Process Lifecycle and reviewed. Further, a concept matrix is conducted in order to give an overview of the current Green BPM tools and techniques according to their provided objectives.

4.1   Green BPM Approaches

In the field of Green Business Process Management there exist only a handful of approaches with regards to sustainable process management. ARDAGNA ET AL. (2008) developed mechanisms for energy-aware resource allocation and policies for process-based applications while ensuring certain Quality of Service (QoS) requirements. Therefore, three layers (process, infrastructure and control) should be capable of decreasing the energy consumption in information and communication technology (ICT). The approach has been further refined in CAPPIELLO ET AL. (2011) who proposed an approach for designing *Energy-Aware Business Process (E-BP)* by extending the typical business process conceptual model to capture the energy consumption of the involved business activities, which is constantly monitored by *Green Performance Indicators* (GPIs) such as Energy Consumption, CO2 Footprint, Recycling, Waste and Water Consumption, that have to be satisfied together with the more functional and non-functional requirements (QoS).

NOWAK ET AL. (2011) used ecological sustainable adaptation patterns *(Green Business Process Patterns)* in order to provide a broad applicability of patterns within different scenarios of sustainability. However, their application affected the business process layer, the application component and the infrastructure layer which is why they also needed Cloud Patterns to guide developers through the adaptation process (Nowak et al. 2012). Later, the study was extended to help organisational stakeholders identifying patterns of their interests and design environmentally-aware business processes (Nowak and Leymann 2013). Another approach in the field of pattern-based business process management was done by LÜEBECKE ET AL. (2016). They identified environmental weaknesses of processes from existing literature and process models and used the concept of Ecological Workflow Patterns (EWPs) to formalize these weaknesses. As a result, they have created four initial EWPs from control-flow, data and operational perspective that serve as a blueprint for the development of environmentally sustainable processes at design time or to optimize existing processes. Later, they extended the study to the concept of *sustainability patterns*, which can be used to improve existing processes or to design new processes by considering environmental objectives such as the reduction of resource consumption (Lübbecke et al. 2017).

ZHU ET AL. (2015) developed an approach which allows the integration of process models with *Geographic Information Systems* (GIS) by applying it to an ecological focused case. Goldkuhl and Lind (2010) present an extended process modelling approach to capture and document the greenhouse gas (GHG) emissions produced during the execution of a business process as well as an accordant analysis method. An integration model for the energy consumption of IT components and business processes increases the transparency of the energy consumption of administrative business processes and enables energy savings. Furthermore, a prototype can be used to develop and validate effective methods for creating energy-efficient business processes (Reiter et al. 2014). WESUMPERUMA ET AL. (2011) derived a framework for multi-dimensional business process optimization which is used for the mitigation of GHG emissions. BETZ (2014) gives a short overview about sustainability aware process management using XML-nets in order to improve sustainability in business processes and therefore the organizational performance (*Extensions of process modelling notations*). HOESCH-KLOHE ET AL. (2010) show that BPMN can also be extended with qualitative annotations such as *emission annotation*. To do this, they have introduced a mechanism, called *ProcessSeer*, so that the carbon emission value of the entire process design can be calculated and be able to perform semantic effect annotations for process models. For the identification of green or environmental waste, R.T. WHITE AND JAMES (2014) proposed an approach to extended process mapping *(Pmapping)*. This method is useful for organizations that want to prioritize their efforts in improving their environmental performance and, at the same time, as an excellent source of information to demonstrate and document the organization's commitment to environmental issues.

CLEVEN ET AL. (2012) discuss the capabilities required to measure and manage sustainability performance on a process level by providing a *capability maturity model (CMM)* for green process performance management capabilities. LARSCH ET AL. (2017) introduced a *process model* which deals with an approach integrating sustainability aspects into business process management by involving a catalogue to support the identification of improvement potentials and its execution.

GHOSE ET AL. (2010) classified resources according their environmental impact and on how they can be reduced during the design of a business process by identifying all relevant carbon emitting entities and combining bottom-up and top-down principles. In a top-down approach, the principles of Activity Based Costing are used to identify contributions from each task to indirect CO2 emissions. The determination of carbon emissions is carried out using the bottom-up method. Furthermore, *Green Activity Based Management* is an approach to green sustainable business process management that extends the principles of Activity Based Costing (ABC) and Critical Path Method (CPM) to capture, measure, model, and report on GHG emissions, while considering the factors of cost and time (Wesumperuma et al. 2013). RECKER ET AL. (2011, 2012) proposed an approach for capturing and documenting the CO2 emissions produced during the execution of a business process which also extends activity-based costing approaches towards the consideration of GHG emissions alongside the activities of a business process (*Activity-Based Emission*). Thereby, it facilitates the consideration of environmental sustainability consideration in the improvement or redesign of business processes. In the study later, they added another approach for measuring the carbon dioxide emissions produced during the execution of a business process (Recker et al. 2012).

NOWAK ET AL. (2011) proposed a four-layered architecture and four-phase *process viewing* methodology to empower organizations defining environmental characteristics, capturing and measuring these environmental characteristics, identifying, localizing, and visualizing their environment and developing appropriate adaptation strategies in order to optimize their environmental impact without neglecting the competitiveness of the organization. The presented architecture describes the fundamental layers needed for a more sustainable organizational environment in the overarching concerns of Green Business Process Reengineering (see Section 4.3).

To address the environmental impact of business processes, a multi-level methodology guides stakeholders through the process of identifying the resources of a business process, defines environmental characterization metrics and their corresponding metrology as well as computational specifications, and disseminates this information to the business process levels. For this, Nowak et al. (2013) used *Enterprise Topology Graphs*.

The *Abnoba framework* is a popular tool in BPM which supports the integration of environmental sustainability aspects of processes (Hoesch-Klohe and Ghose 2010). For this, HOESCH-KLOHE AND GHOSE (2011) extended the framework by introducing and elaborating a machinery for (semi-)automated process redesign discovery. The machinery uses a library of process fragments, which is used to replace library fragments with process design fragments, so that process redesign meets functionality, process delivery, and compliance requirements and improves the sustainability profile (Houy et al. 2012).

LÜBBECKE ET AL. (2015) presented an approach for applying *Business Process Simulation* (BPS) techniques, using established simulation software that also supports the analysis of path complexities of business process models, thus preparing for effective decision-making in an environmental context.

4.2 Mapping into the Lifecycle

SEIDEL ET AL. (2012) identified the requirement to extend the traditional BPM Lifecycle into a Green BPM Lifecycle. For this reason, the Lifecycle introduced by DUMAS ET AL. (2013) is chosen and adapted according to a more sustainable context (Fig. 4):

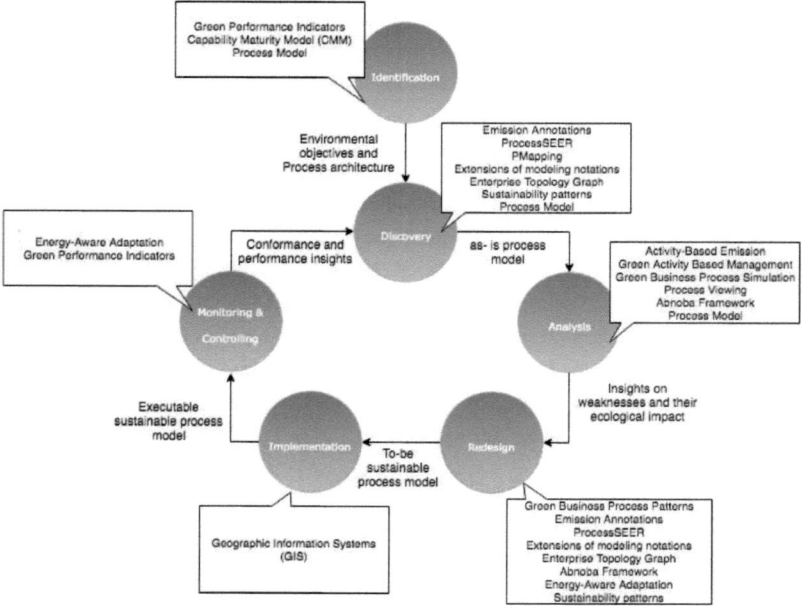

Dumas et al. (2013), p. 21

Fig. 4 Green BPM Lifecycle

Looking into the adapted Green Business Process Lifecycle[1], all the tools and techniques mentioned in the previous subsection can be mapped into it. In the course of this, each approach was entered in the relevant phases of the Lifecycle according to its procedure. Some approaches just fit into one phase like the Capability Maturity Model (into the identification phase) thus its major objective is just providing capabilities required for the later measuring and monitoring of ecological performance (Cleven et al. 2012). But there are also approaches which can be entered into multiple phases. For instance, the process model proposed by LARSCH ET AL. (2017) can fit into the identification, discovery as well

---

[1] A more detailed overview of the categorization is given in the Appendix

as analysis phase hence it should facilitate the integration of sustainability aspects into business processes with providing a catalogue and supports the stakeholders from the idea generation to model analysis. It is very noticeable that the redesign phase is covered by the most approaches and the implementation phase is nearly ignored.

4.3 Four application areas of Green BPM approaches

In order to give a more detailed interpretation of the results, the approaches are classified into four distinct application areas according to GOHAR AND INDULSKA (2015): Process Performance Measurement Method Extension, Process Modelling Extension, Process Reengineering and Design as well as Process Optimization (Tab. 1). The range of performance measurement extension refers to developed and adopted performance measurement approaches which capture the environmental process performance. The modelling extension refers to additional modelling elements in process modelling notations and architectures to enrich process models with sustainability concepts. Process reengineering and design deal with approaches that help organizations to design and reengineer their business processes based on environmental objectives such as reducing CO_2 or GHG emissions. Process optimization considers the redesign, improvement and adoption of developed concepts for business processes in iterative steps towards sustainable goals.

	Performance Measurement	Modelling Extensions	Reengineering and Design	Optimization
CMM	√			
GPI	√			√
GIS			√	
Emission Annotations	√	√		
Abnoba	√		√	
GBPM Patterns				√
Activity-Based-Emission	√	√		
ProcessSEER	√			
PMapping		√		
Extensions		√		√
Enterprise Topology Graphs			√	√
Sustainability Patterns			√	
Green Activity Based Management	√			
Process Viewing	√			
Energy-aware Adaptation		√	√	
Simulation			√	

Tab. 1   Application areas of Green BPM approaches

As seen in the table, some approaches are applicable to more than one area. This has to do with the fact that these approaches have several objectives that they include. For instance, they can be extensions of regular modelling approaches and at the same time they could also look for performance measurements.

According to GOHAR AND INDULSKA (2015), approaches in the field of Process Performance Measurement are mostly used than other BPM concepts. There are several studies that focus on measuring and managing indicators such as energy usage, CO_2 and GHG emissions. However, it is also necessary to examine the applicability, change, and impact on organizational performance after implementing such techniques and measurement methods. Taking into account the industry to stop climate change and reduce emissions, Green BPM studies require the implementation of measurement methods and the necessary planning of organizational processes. Process modelling notations are ideal for reflecting indicators such as CO_2 or GHG emissions. However, further research is needed to suggest the applicability of these notations in practice. The application of Business Process Reengineering, Design and Optimization requires further studies regarding the applicability of the approaches in practice and the possible implementation success. There are still possible factors to implement eco-friendlier processes. However, as Devil's Pentagon's existing trade-offs make it difficult to plan, introduce and implement environmental sustainability concepts (in conjunction with higher costs and significant changes), future research must focus in particular on the successful implementation and validation of Green BPM approaches. At this point, studies to introduce guidance on greener processes would be very important.

5   Discussion

This section reflects the main contributions presented in the previous chapter and thus evaluates on which degree Green BPM approaches are extensions of regular BPM approaches.

There exist only a few approaches in the literature that explicitly discuss and address business processes as a way to improve a company's environmental impact (Ghose et al. 2010; Seidel et al. 2012). The few existing approaches only relate to individual parts of Business Process Management. For example, they focus on the energy efficiency of IT systems or the quantification of all relevant environmental influences. The design of a comprehensive BPM, which includes both the traditional optimization aspects and the environmental impact, must be accomplished. This leads to the problem of the Devil's Pentagon, in which the aspect of sustainability is inserted, but its existence can negatively affect the other dimensions such as costs (Ghose et al. 2010). Of course, the reason may be that the approaches only cover particular parts of the (Green) BPM Lifecycle. For example, some approaches, such as CMM and GIS, only consider individual phases of the Lifecycle without really providing connectivity to other phases. Although their tasks lie in the identification or implementation of the business process, the transition to other phases remains untouched. This may eventually result in increased costs due to mismatch of different approaches. However, other techniques are great for integration with other approaches. Thus, Green Performance Indicators are well suited to integrate into Energy-Aware Adaptation since it can be used for the monitoring of processes and supporting sustainable adaptation. Or the mechanism of the ProcessSEER, which can be useful for extending BPMN through emission annotation. However, these connection points of several techniques and tools are sporadically observed in the literature because they do not cover the entire scope. Furthermore, there are some approaches who fit into more than one phase of the Lifecycle. Particularly striking here is that the approaches are assigned exactly in the phases of discovery, analysis and redesign. In particular, the redesign phase is covered by most of the techniques and tools. This may have to do with the fact that the concepts already existed in previous BPM works and only adapted to sustainability aspects. The redesign phase deals with the identification and transformation of process changes in cooperation with the previous phase of analysis (Dumas et al. 2013). This may be the reason why these approaches are considered in the analysis and redesign phase thus they have to work together through multiple iterative steps to improve an already existing business process. In addition, the strong focus on redesign can be explained by the fact that the BPM experts use their approaches to insert the dimension of sustainability into their processes. They adapt already existing approaches to ecological values, so that the business process is finally reshaped. Only at the point of implementation is a whole series of work still missing. Thus researchers have focused only on the analysis and the transformation of existing business processes towards more sustainability, which is why the implementation is still missing in practice. This can be observed in the small number of applied techniques (see GIS).

In contrast to the case allocation in the conventional BPM Lifecycle proposed by VOM BROCKE AND MENDLING (2018), the Green BPM Lifecycle in this thesis deals with much less phases of implementation and much more in terms of process analysis. This also clarifies the fact that the focus of Green BPM approaches lies on the configuration and transformation of current tools and techniques whereas implementing the concepts into a business context is nearly not given. Of course, the analysis and redesign phases are in interaction with each other which emphasizes the importance of reengineering current processes.

At the very most, it can be said that Green BPM approaches consist of aspects already presented in BPM which are further adapted to sustainability aspects. New tools and techniques were not developed in any of the cases. The majority of studies are contributions in the early stages of development, with only a limited number of studies validating their approaches. Of course, there have to be much more approaches in the research in order to give better prediction. In addition, it must be put into practice, since most approaches were only used in research. Therefore, further investigations are required.

Thus Green BPM is still in its early stages, there are not many approaches which deal with new techniques and tools. Instead, existing approaches are used and adapted to sustainable objectives. Although these approaches are applied in the research context, they lack in practice hence their significance is still questionable. Therefore, it should be noted that the approaches in their usage for practical matter are not yet far advanced and there is still room for improvement here. Therefore, in future research projects, it would be possible to rely more on the design of new approaches including new tools and techniques so that different phases of the (Green) BPM Lifecycle such as the implementation or identification phases are also addressed.

6   Holistic consideration

The aim of this work was to find relevant approaches of Green BPM and analyse them with regard to their purpose. It was considered whether the approaches are extensions of the traditional BPM concepts adapted to the ecological dimension or if they are newer techniques and tools introduced by the rise of Green IS. In order to achieve this goal, the basic concept of BPM and its way towards more sustainability was presented at the beginning followed by the explanation of current approaches. Afterwards, the BPM Lifecycle, which serves as a suitable framework to allocate the different tools and techniques, was introduced. Based on the rough presentation, the main part deals more intensively and in more detail with the tools and techniques of Green BPM approaches. These tools and techniques were mapped into an adapted (Green) BPM Lifecycle so that relevant implications could be derived in the discussion section. But first, the mentioned tools and techniques were classified according their field of acting. Finally, the discussion part took place where the major contributions were analysed and interpreted according to the observed results and background knowledge.

References

Ardagna, D., Cappiello, C., Lovera, M., Pernici, B., and Tanelli, M. 2008. *Active Energy-Aware Management of Business-Process Based Applications.*

Betz, S. 2014. "Sustainability Aware Process Management using XML-Nets," p. 8.

vom Brocke, J., and Mendling, J. 2018. "Frameworks for Business Process Management: A Taxonomy for Business Process Management Cases," in *Business Process Management Cases: Digital Innovation and Business Transformation in Practice*, J. vom Brocke and J. Mendling (eds.), Cham: Springer International Publishing, pp. 1–17.

Bucher, T., Raber, D., and Winter, R. 2015. "A Taxonomy of Business Process Management Approaches," in *Handbook on Business Process Management 2: Strategic Alignment, Governance, People and Culture*, J. vom Brocke and M. Rosemann (eds.), Berlin, Heidelberg: Springer Berlin Heidelberg, pp. 203–225.

Cappiello, C., Fugini, M., Ferreira, A. M., Plebani, P., and Vitali, M. 2011. "Business process co-design for energy-aware adaptation," IEEE, pp. 463–470.

Cleven, A., Winter, R., and Wortmann, F. 2012. "Managing Process Performance to Enable Corporate Sustainability: A Capability Maturity Model," in *Green Business Process Management: Towards the Sustainable Enterprise*, J. vom Brocke, S. Seidel and J. Recker (eds.), Berlin, Heidelberg: Springer Berlin Heidelberg, pp. 111–129.

Dumas, M., La Rosa, M., Mendling, J., and Reijers, H. A. 2013. *Fundamentals of Business Process Management*, Berlin, Heidelberg: Springer Berlin Heidelberg.

Ghose, A., Hoesch-Klohe, K., Hinsche, L., and Le, L.-S. 2010. "GREEN BUSINESS PROCESS MANAGEMENT: A RESEARCH AGENDA," *Australasian Journal of Information Systems* (16:2).

Gohar, S. R., and Indulska, M. 2015. "Business Process Management: Saving the Planet?," p. 14.

Goldkuhl, G., and Lind, M. 2010. "A Multi-Grounded Design Research Process," in *Global Perspectives on Design Science Research*, R. Winter, J.L. Zhao and S. Aier (eds.), Springer Berlin Heidelberg, pp. 45–60.

Hammer, M., and Champy, J. 1993. "Reengineering the corporation: A manifesto for business revolution," *Business Horizons* (36:5), pp. 90–91.

Hoesch-Klohe, K., Ghose, A., and Lê, L.-S. 2010. "Towards Green Business Process Management," IEEE, pp. 386–393.

Hoesch-Klohe, K., and Ghose, A. 2010. "Carbon-Aware Business Process Design in Abnoba," in *Service-Oriented Computing*, P.P. Maglio, M. Weske, J. Yang and M. Fantinato (eds.), Berlin, Heidelberg: Springer Berlin Heidelberg, pp. 551–556.

Hoesch-Klohe, K., and Ghose, A. 2011. "Business Process Improvement in Abnoba," in *Service-Oriented Computing*, E.M. Maximilien, G. Rossi, S.-T. Yuan, H. Ludwig and M. Fantinato (eds.), Berlin, Heidelberg: Springer Berlin Heidelberg, pp. 193–202.

Houy, C., Reiter, M., Fettke, P., Loos, P. 2010. Towards Green BPM - Sustainability and Resource Efficiency through Business Process Management. In Business Process Management Workshops.

Houy, C., Reiter, M., Fettke, P., Loos, P., Hoesch-Klohe, K., and Ghose, A. 2012. *Advancing Business Process Technology for Humanity - Opportunities and Challenges of Green BPM for Sustainable Business Activities.*

J.-P. Pritchard and C. Armistead 1999. Business process management - Lessons from European business, Business Process Management Journal. Volume 5, Number I

Karagiannis, D. 2013. "Business Process Management: A Holistic Management Approach," in *Information Systems: Methods, Models, and Applications*, H.C. Mayr, C. Kop, S. Liddle and A. Ginige (eds.), Berlin, Heidelberg: Springer Berlin Heidelberg, pp. 1–12.

Larsch, S., Betz, S., Duboc, L., Magdaleno, A. M., and Bomfim, C. 2017. "Integrating Sustainability Aspects in Business Process Management," in *Business Process Management Workshops*, M. Dumas and M. Fantinato (eds.), Springer International Publishing, pp. 403–415.

Levy, Y., and J. Ellis, T. 2006. "A Systems Approach to Conduct an Effective Literature Review in Support of Information Systems Research," *Informing Science: The International Journal of an Emerging Transdiscipline* (9), pp. 181–212.

Lübbecke, P., Fettke, P., and Loos, P. 2017. "Sustainability Patterns for the Improvement of IT-Related Business Processes with Regard to Ecological Goals," in *Business Process Management Workshops*, M. Dumas and M. Fantinato (eds.), Springer International Publishing, pp. 428–439.

Lubbecke, P., Fettke, P., and Loos, P. 2016. "Towards Ecological Workflow Patterns as an Instrument to Optimize Business Processes with Respect to Ecological Goals," IEEE, pp. 1049–1058.

Lubbecke, P., Reiter, M., Fettke, P., and Loos, P. 2015. "Simulation-Based Decision Support for the Reduction of the Energy Consumption of Complex Business Processes," IEEE, pp. 866–875.

Mansar, S. L., and Reijers, H. A. 2005. "Best practices in business process redesign: validation of a redesign framework," *Computers in Industry* (56:5), pp. 457–471.

M.J. Melenovsky, Business Process Management as a Discipline 2006. Gartner Research, GOO139856 (Gartner Inc.)

Møller, C., Maack, C. J., and Tan, R. D. 2008. "What is Business Process Management: A Two Stage Literature Review of an Emerging Field," in *Research and Practical Issues of Enterprise Information Systems II Volume 1*, L.D. Xu, A.M. Tjoa and S.S. Chaudhry (eds.), Boston, MA: Springer US, pp. 19–31.

Nowak, A., Binz, T., Leymann, F., and Urbach, N. 2013. "Determining Power Consumption of Business Processes and Their Activities to Enable Green Business Process Reengineering," IEEE, pp. 259–266.

Nowak, A., Leymann, F., Schleicher, D., Schumm, D., and Wagner, S. 2011. *Green Business Process Patterns*.

Nowak, A., Leymann, F., Schumm, D., and Wetzstein, B. 2011. "An Architecture and Methodology for a Four-Phased Approach to Green Business Process Reengineering," in *Information and Communication on Technology for the Fight against Global Warming*, D. Kranzlmüller and A.M. Toja (eds.), Berlin, Heidelberg: Springer Berlin Heidelberg, pp. 150–164.

Nowak, A., and Leymann, F. 2013. "Green Business Process Patterns -- Part II (Short Paper)," IEEE, pp. 168–173.

Opitz, N., Langkau, T.F., Erek, K., Kolbe, L.M., Zarnekow, R. (2012). Kick-starting Green Business Process Management – Suitable Modeling Languages and Key Processes for Green Performance Measurement. American Conference on Informations Systems 2012, Seattle, USA.

Opitz, N., Krüp, H., Kolbe, L.M. 2014. Green Business Process Management – A Definition and Research Framework. In 47th Hawaii International Conference on System Science

P. Redshaw 2005. How Banks Can Benefit from Business Process Management, Gartner Research, GOO126515

Recker, J., Rosemann, M., and Gohar, E. R. 2011. "Measuring the Carbon Footprint of Business Processes," in *Business Process Management Workshops*, M. zur Muehlen and J. Su (eds.), Springer Berlin Heidelberg, pp. 511–520.

Recker, J., Rosemann, M., Hjalmarsson, A., and Lind, M. 2012. "Modeling and Analyzing the Carbon Footprint of Business Processes," in *Green Business Process Management: Towards the Sustainable Enterprise*, J. vom Brocke, S. Seidel and J. Recker (eds.), Berlin, Heidelberg: Springer Berlin Heidelberg, pp. 93–109.

Reiter, M., Fettke, P., and Loos, P. 2014. "Towards Green Business Process Management: Concept and Implementation of an Artifact to Reduce the Energy Consumption of Business Processes," IEEE, pp. 885–894.

Rohloff, M. 2011. "Advances in business process management implementation based on a maturity assessment and best practice exchange," *Information Systems and e-Business Management* (9:3), pp. 383–403.

R.G. Lee and B.G. Dale (1998). Business Process management: a review and evaluation, Business Process Management Journal. Volume 4, Number 3, pp. 2] 4-225

R.T. White, G., and James, P. 2014. "Extension of process mapping to identify 'green waste,'" *Benchmarking: An International Journal* (21:5), pp. 835–850.

Scheer, A.-W. 2015. "The Process of Business Process Management". In Handbook on Business Process Management. Springer Verlag - Berlin, Jan vom Brocke, Michael Rosemann (eds.). pp. 351-380

Seidel, S., Recker, J., and vom Brocke, J. 2012. "Green Business Process Management," in *Green Business Process Management*, J vom Brocke, S. Seidel and J. Recker (eds.), Berlin, Heidelberg: Springer Berlin Heidelberg, pp. 3–13.

Staubus, G.J.: Activity Costing and Input-Output Accounting (1971)

vom Brocke, J., Schmiedel, T., Recker, J., Trkman, P., Mertens, W., & Viaene, S. (2014). Ten principles of good business process management. Business Process Management Journal (BPMJ), 20(4), 530–548.

Watson, R. T., Boudreau, M. C. and Chen, A.J. (2010) Information Systems and Environmentally Sustainable Development: Energy Informatics and New Directions for the IS Community, MIS Quarterly, 34, 1, 22- 38.

Webster, J., and Watson, R. T. "Guest Editorial: Analyzing the Past to Prepare for the Future: Writing a literature Review," p. 11.

Wesumperuma, A., Ginige, A., Ginige, J. A., and Hol, A. 2013. "Green Activity Based Management (ABM) for Organisations," p. 11.

Wesumperuma, A., Ginige, J. A., Ginige, A., and Hol, A. 2011. "A Framework for Multi-dimensional Business Process Optimization for GEG Emission Mitigation," p. 11.

Zhu, X., Zhu, G., vanden Broucke, S., and Recker, J. 2015. "On Merging Business Process Management and Geographic Information Systems: Modeling and Execution of Ecological Concerns in Processes," in *Geo-Informatics in Resource Management and Sustainable Ecosystem*, F. Bian and Y. Xie (eds.), Berlin, Heidelberg: Springer Berlin Heidelberg, pp. 486–496.

Appendix

A   Additional information

BPM/IS search terms	Boolean Operators	Sustainability terms	Boolean Operators	Specifying terms
Business Process Management (BPM)	AND/ NEAR	Green	AND/ NEAR	Approach
Information Systems (IS)		Environment*		Tools
Process		Sustain*		Techniques
		Emission		
		Energy		
		Ecological		
		Carbon*		

Tab. 2   Keywords

	Identification	Discovery	Analysis	Redesign	Implementation	Monitoring & Control
GPI	√	X	X	X	X	√
CMM	√	X	X	X	X	X
GIS	X	X	X	X	√	X
Emission Annotations	X	√	X	√	X	X
Abnoba	X	X	√	√	X	X
GBPM Patterns	X	X	X	√	X	X
Activity-Based-Emission	X	X	√	X	X	X
ProcessSEER	X	√	X	√	X	X
PMapping	X	√	X		X	X
Extensions	X	√	X	√	X	X
Enterprise Topology Graph	X	√	X	√	X	X
Sustainability Patterns	X	√	X	√	X	X
Green Activity Based Management	X	X	√	X	X	X
Process Viewing	X	X	√	X	X	X
Energy-Aware Adaptation	X	X		√	X	√
Simulation	X	X	√	X	X	X
Process Model	√	√	√	X	X	X
Σ	3	7	6	8	1	2

Tab. 3   Allocation of Tools and Techniques to the BPM Lifecycle

YOUR KNOWLEDGE HAS VALUE